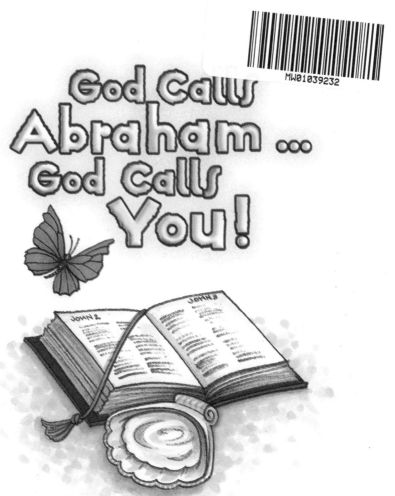

God Calls Abraham ... God Calls You!

Genesis 12:1–9; Isaiah 43:1 for children

Melinda Kay Busch
Illustrated by Michelle Dorenkamp

Arch® Books
Copyright © 2003 Concordia Publishing House
3558 S. Jefferson Avenue, St. Louis, MO 63118-3968
Manufactured in Colombia

The Lord spoke out to Abraham
And called on him by name.
"Leave your people and the land
To which your father came.

"I will show you where to go,
Be with you as you roam;
I will set apart a land
To be your people's home.

"I'll make you a great nation,
Your name will be great too.
Those who bless you I will bless,
And curse those who curse you.

"All the peoples of the earth
Will be blessed through you.
I make this promise, Abraham,
And My promises are true."

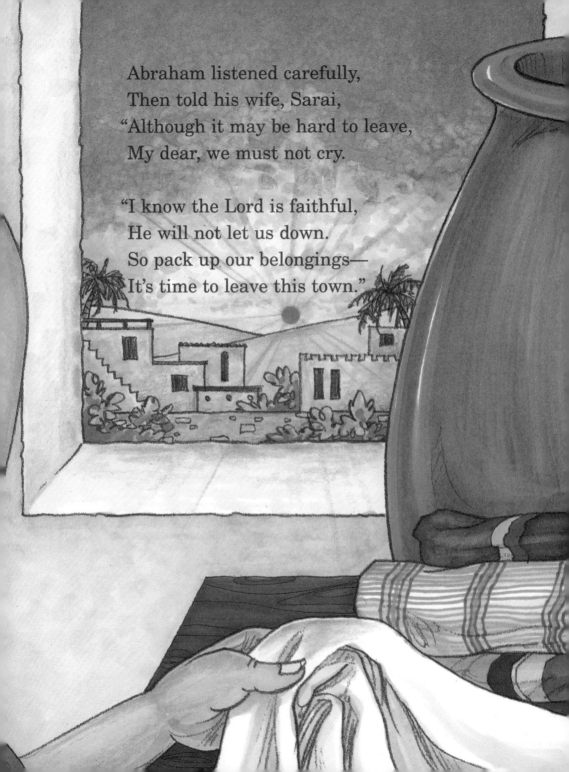

Abraham listened carefully,
Then told his wife, Sarai,
"Although it may be hard to leave,
My dear, we must not cry.

"I know the Lord is faithful,
He will not let us down.
So pack up our belongings—
It's time to leave this town."

Abraham left as he was told,
And set upon his way.
He journeyed across Canaan,
To the great tree of Moreh.

There the Lord Himself appeared,
And gestured all around.
"Abraham, look upon this land,
Study well this ground!

"For your children and for theirs
I promise all these lands."
Abraham built an altar there
To God with his own hands.

For many years he wondered
When God would keep His word;
Abraham did not have a son,
But yet he served the Lord.

At last came baby Isaac,
And Isaac had two sons.
Then Jacob had a host of twelve!
The list had just begun!

Many long years came and went,
And then a special Son
Was born inside a stable—
He was the Holy One.

Jesus came into our world
To take away our sin.
He died then rose on Easter,
Our life with God to win.

And so God kept His promise—
The peoples of the earth
Were truly blessed through Abraham
When Jesus had His birth.

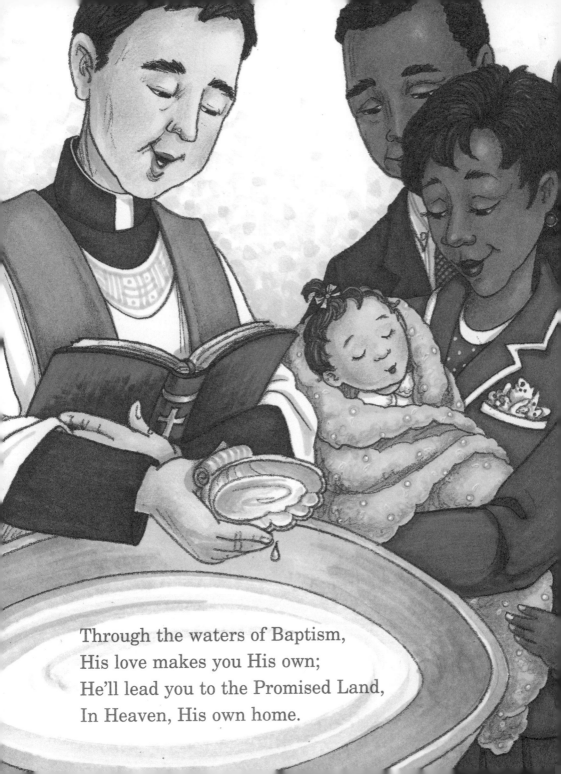

Through the waters of Baptism,
His love makes you His own;
He'll lead you to the Promised Land,
In Heaven, His own home.

Now, just as God called Abraham,
He's also calling you
To go the way He's chosen—
His Word is always true!

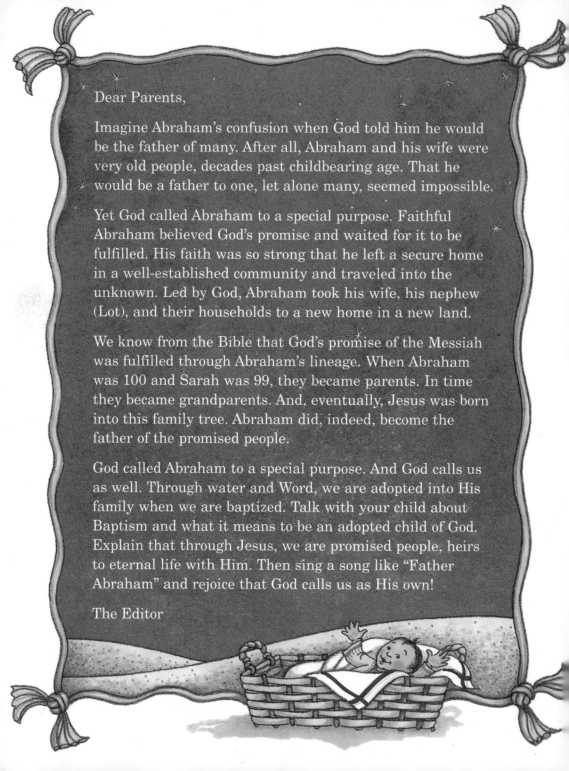

Dear Parents,

Imagine Abraham's confusion when God told him he would be the father of many. After all, Abraham and his wife were very old people, decades past childbearing age. That he would be a father to one, let alone many, seemed impossible.

Yet God called Abraham to a special purpose. Faithful Abraham believed God's promise and waited for it to be fulfilled. His faith was so strong that he left a secure home in a well-established community and traveled into the unknown. Led by God, Abraham took his wife, his nephew (Lot), and their households to a new home in a new land.

We know from the Bible that God's promise of the Messiah was fulfilled through Abraham's lineage. When Abraham was 100 and Sarah was 99, they became parents. In time they became grandparents. And, eventually, Jesus was born into this family tree. Abraham did, indeed, become the father of the promised people.

God called Abraham to a special purpose. And God calls us as well. Through water and Word, we are adopted into His family when we are baptized. Talk with your child about Baptism and what it means to be an adopted child of God. Explain that through Jesus, we are promised people, heirs to eternal life with Him. Then sing a song like "Father Abraham" and rejoice that God calls us as His own!

The Editor